TEEN-AGER
YOUR
CHURCH
IS
FOR
YOU

Then His mother and His brothers arrived to see Him, but could not get near Him because of the crowd. So a message was passed to Him,

"Your mother and Your brothers are standing outside wanting to see You."

To which He replied,

"My mother and My brothers? That means those who listen to God's message and obey it."

LUKE 8:19-21 *(Phillips)*

TEEN-AGER

YOUR

CHURCH

IS

FOR

YOU

By Walter Riess

CONCORDIA PUBLISHING HOUSE
SAINT LOUIS, MISSOURI

Concordia Publishing House, Saint Louis 18, Missouri
Concordia Publishing House Ltd., London, W. C. 1.
Copyright 1961 by Concordia Publishing House
Library of Congress Catalog Card No. 60-53153

Third Printing 1963

Manufactured in the United States of America

For Judy

HOW YOUR CHURCH LOVES YOU

THE HAPPIEST THING
THAT EVER HAPPENED

The holy Christian church is, next to Jesus Christ, the most delightful thing that can happen to any teen-ager.

I can say this and know what I'm talking about. Because the Christian church is the happiest thing that ever happened to me, bar none.

Some of my teen friends might rib me, right about now, by saying that my life might look something like an 1890 parlor. But I have seen enough of this streamlined chrome-polished century to know that even the most up-to-date lives can be unified and blessed by the church.

In fact, it is exactly *because* our age glitters so gaudily and rushes so madly that we need to look into ourselves, shudder a minute, and then risk the question:

Teen-ager, just where do you think you *are* going?

This makes a horrendously painful question for our anxious chrome-plated minds. We have to dent through layers of civilized lies just to ask it, really ask it, and get any kind of answer beyond a muffled squeak. It is not good to be alone, and we never know that better than when we try to find out for ourselves just who we are — and what we are trying to do with our lives — and hardest of all, *why*.

And right at that moment when we stand most alone, we may come to realize that the church has more meaning for us today than it had for the parlor rooms of 1890. Like eagles with injured wings we may rise to her out of sheer driving need and find in her not only who God is — but who we are: teen-agers, yes, and a thousand times more than that: redeemed children of our Lord, called to Him and sent out to be the kind of people only He can make.

That's why your church can be the most propelling thing that ever happened to you. Because your own Lord and your own people wait for you there to help you see *exactly* who you are and where you are going.

We want to help you *see yourself* — under heaven.

WHAT IF WE DON'T
FEEL WE "BELONG"?

Exactly how do you "see yourself"?

Do you feel when you walk through your church doors on a Sunday morning that you are with your people? Or do you feel bored, maybe even angry that you have to be going to church — and maybe even afraid that the people and the minister do not really appreciate your kind of person?

Every teen-ager at one time or another has to face in himself some negative feelings about church, because church can spell a-u-t-h-o-r-i-t-y, and teen-agers, almost automatically, like an alarm clock going off, feel an inner revulsion against authority. This leads to something even worse — a feeling of not being wanted or loved by the church.

Most of us, in plain English, do not realize how much God loves us.

And that, in one sentence, explains 99 9/10% of our unhappiness.

Members of my Sunday morning teen circle look out over fields gray with frost or green with springtime. Our room looks over the crest of a country slope so that we have below us a spread of sunlight enough to inspire a gopher. Inside the room we read and talk about the soaring pages of the Gospels. We try to see what all these days of the Galilee Savior can mean to teen-agers.

Surrounded by all this radiance, we still stammer nonsense. *"How can God love me if . . .?"* *"No one's interested in my problems."* *"Don't ask the congregation for anything — they don't want to bother with us."* *"My parents don't understand me, and there's no use talking about it. It won't help."*

That still leaves about 97% of our feelings in us — feelings rotting deep underneath. Feelings of being unwanted, unloved, of not belonging — *not even to the church.*

Where is the Shepherd's voice now? "My sheep

hear My voice, and I know them, and they follow Me," He said. But we can't hear. And how can we follow a voice we can't hear?

This is a contrast to shake our souls — the difference between Christ's voice over the sands of Galilee and the high-pitched hum of a church loudspeaker. We get snagged on differences like that. Suddenly we find ourselves wondering whether the church today has anything at all to do with the Christ of love.

But believe it or not, even this *wondering* is part of hearing the voice of Christ.

He doesn't send angels with pink trumpets. He puts a free and open question box into your cranium. He guides you into a family and a group of people called a Christian congregation. And He says, "Ask your questions — right here, *with My people to help you on to answers!"*

People — of all things!

Farmers and scrubwomen and assembly-line workers — answer *my* questions?

Exactly. Just like the fishermen who wrote a fine part of our New Testament.

Peter wasn't writing to anyone's board of directors when he said this: *"But you are the elect race, the royal priesthood, the consecrated nation, the People who belong to Him . . ."* (Moffatt). He was writing to people in Asia Minor — teen-agers too — who had to fight hard just to stay out of temples where sex sins were the order of the day! These were "the People who belong to Him."

They did their share of wondering too when they read *this* letter, the first of Peter's two in the New Testament. Maybe *they* took to wishing that Christ would come back and escort them visibly and easily into the golden gates.

But He didn't.
He gave them Peter, a pastor.
And He gave them people.

Where are your people?
Yes, they do love you. Yes, they are bad at showing it. Yes, they do want to help you. Yes, they don't always know how.

But find them, find your people.
Your Savior — the same Galilean — has worked His wonders in them. They own His Gospel.

Somehow, if you stay with them through all the muddling efforts of these beloved people of God — somehow you'll feel His love on you. You will feel His hand.

You *will*.

HE'S THE CENTER
OF YOUR LIFE

Enjoying church is enjoying people.
It is feeling that you belong to
people.

It is even more feeling that you
belong to one particular Person, the
most magnificent Hero who ever
lived. And the real happy thing
about this Hero is that He still
lives for you.

Suppose for a minute that Jesus
were to rise today. Pretend that
all the news services — United
Press, Wide World, Telenews, As-
sociated Press, and all the rest —
got hold of the story. Where do

you think the write-up would be printed — on page three or page one?

Would it take the headlines or the back-page picture section? Would it make the TV network or only the local radio news?

You couldn't escape the story. It would follow you wherever you went. It would challenge you to believe, or doubt, or deny. *But it wouldn't let you alone!*

That's the way it is with this miraculous, all-conquering Jesus Christ.

No one like Him has ever lived or ever will live on earth again. He's over all history and all science, all geography and all men's thoughts. He's *God!*

He is the Center of everything.

He is the Center of everything in the church too.

All the teachings, or doctrines, of this church may seem a little confusing — until you trace each one down to Him. Until you see that each one of these teachings is only like the handgrip on a ship's pilot wheel. We can use this grip or that to steer the ship, but the wheel itself is Jesus Christ.

That makes Jesus much more than *one* of the doctrines of the church. That makes Him THE ONLY DOCTRINE. He is the real power behind all that Christians say or do or believe. He still is the wheel that steers the whole ship.

That's why Jesus is still Treasure upon Treasure to millions of people all over the world today: because He still enriches their lives with the treasure of the Gospel of forgiveness. Because He still lights up their saddest hours with the hope of His miracles. Because He still answers prayers. Because He still stands at the center of everything.

If you remember Jesus when you think about the church and the teachings of the church, you will be able to keep clearer about everything. You will be able to keep your head up above the confusion of the world around you too. For Christ is the answer to that problem also. And His love for you is enough to keep you for Himself.

He is still talking to you.

He is still saying, *"I am the Way, the Truth, and the Life,"* just to you.

And when you hear Him say that — just to you — the world of Christian doctrine dawns into light for you. You awake to the fact that every doctrine is His gift to you and proves His love for you, His care for you, His eternal desire to have you for His own, to be the Center of *your* life.

So there are many doctrines but only one Doctrine; many teachings but only one Teaching. They all end up with Jesus Christ. And if you have Him, you have everything.

Do you have Him?

You certainly can, and I think you do. That's why you are wondering now about living your life with Jesus.

The very fact that you want to live with Him proves: *He is here with you.* And He is.

HOW JESUS CHRIST BRINGS
DOCTRINE TO LIFE

This Hero of ours, Jesus Christ, is not only the Center of the people who belong to your church, He is the Center of the teachings of your church.

Remember our picture of the ship's pilot wheel? Jesus is the wheel itself, and the doctrines are the handgrips by which we turn the wheel.

Right here we could let go of our ship's wheel — and maybe that would be a good idea. But let's hang on for a minute longer.

Suppose you'd taken a hatchet

and chopped off all the handgrips on that wheel. How would you steer a ship without something to grab on to — or would you just let the rudder flap around like a kite in a whirlwind?

That's exactly (believe it or not) what some nice Christian folks do after they get to thinking about their church.

"If Jesus Christ is the heart of our religion, why do we have to bother with all these other things that get so complicated?"

So runs the story.

It's a story you hear often when you get into talks about other churches. Why let a bunch of doctrines keep Christian churches apart? Why not just concentrate on Jesus Christ and forget all the extras?

So simple. So easy. And we're out of all our problems.

— And we may be out of line with Jesus too.

Because He Himself never ignored doctrine. *He* insisted on being baptized. *He* ordained the Lord's Supper. *He* told His friends: "All power in heaven and on earth has been given to Me. You, then, are to go and make disciples of all the nations and *baptize them* in the name of the Father and of the Son and of the Holy Spirit. *Teach them to observe all* that I have commanded you, and remember, I am with you always, even to the end of the world." (Phillips)

See how He Himself hooks Himself up with His doctrines. He says: *"All power is Mine. You baptize. You teach all things."*

There's the secret. Christ's power itself moves through His teachings.

By holding these teachings we hold the Person who gave them to us. We hold on to Jesus!

Let's go back to our ship's wheel again. If you see your pilot guiding the ship, you say, "He's at the wheel." And he is!

So you look at your own soul. You are baptized. You are planning to be confirmed, or you have been confirmed. You want to attend the Lord's Supper.

All this has to do with Jesus' doctrines. And because you are interested in these doctrines, you can be sure that you are "at the wheel." Because your church thinks seriously about doctrine, you can be sure your church takes Jesus seriously too.

You can be absolutely sure that you are one of the Savior's own, because —

> **They go together — Jesus Christ and His teachings.**
> **Take one, and you must take the other.**
> **It's all one wheel, one rudder, one ship.**
> **And it's all for you.**

HOW JESUS LIGHTS UP THE BIBLE

When you hear the word Bible, what do you think of?

The Twenty-third Psalm? Sermon on the Mount? Ten Commandments?

To many good folks this is the real stuff of which our Bible is made. It's like a collection of fancy writings or a book of brightly colored paintings of scenes like the ones on Sunday school leaflets — Israel Crossing the Jordan, Moses on Mount Sinai, Jesus in the Garden.

Now, you wouldn't say these

ideas are far from the mark, would you? There sure are a lot of stories in the Bible, and they do make quite a colorful parade when you line them up one after the other.

But if you stop there, what have you got? An Old Testament history, some incidents from the life of someone who called himself Jesus Christ, some letters by a man named Paul, tinted with a few bits of poetry and colored with Jewish laws.

Many of us never do get either to like or to understand the Bible. It is too big for us, too confusing, too filled with stories and poems and sermons and pictures for us to grab hold of and say: *Here, now I know what it's all about.* After all, even Einstein's formula for freeing atomic energy, as difficult as it is, can be put into a few letters: $E = mc^2$. But the Bible? Who has a formula for that?

Well, maybe somebody *has.*

One of the people who opened up the whole Scripture record in a single paragraph was John — the disciple who grew closer to Jesus than any other person. John said this: "Jesus gave a great many other signs in the presence of His disciples which are not recorded in this book. But *these have been written so that you may believe that Jesus is Christ, the Son of God, and that in that faith you may have life as His followers.*" (John 20:30, 31 Phillips)

Martin Luther called this life "the forgiveness of sins."

That's exactly what the Bible is all about: FORGIVENESS OF SINS, ONCE AND FOREVER GIVEN TO PEOPLE AT CALVARY. And then don't forget to add the next word to it: LIFE. They go together in the Bible — and in the world. You can't really live without forgiveness, without knowing that your own personal Savior has borne your sins and carried your sorrows and your own problems.

You might see your Bible, then, as a slice of the life that a Christian enjoys with his Lord. Or as a sea shell that roars into your ear like the ocean itself. Or as a mirror that shows you not only yourself but the Lord Jesus standing alongside you with His hand holding yours.

This Bible is the one inspired Word which God speaks to you. It is the way He reaches out to you to whisper, "I *do* care about you!" It is — every part of it — a thing from heaven by which your Lord offers Himself to you for now and for always.

Maybe you've heard someone say something like: "Well, I can't believe the Bible can hold everything about God. He must be bigger than a book!" Such a person might toss out the Bible because of a common misunderstanding.

No real Christian says that the Bible "can hold

everything about God." Of course not. God is not bound between two cardboard covers. But we do say that *the Bible tells us everything God wants us to know about Himself.* And we do say that *the Bible tells us how we look to God.*

And in telling us all this, the Bible constantly builds up our spiritual muscle. It isn't only that we're learning something from this book. It's that we're breathing in the spirit of the whole Gospel, and drawing from the faith of those who wrote the record in the first place.

This Bible is like bread. You can eat of it and keep eating and still never finish. The bread stays. Your muscle grows. Your strength increases.

Sounds unbelievable? Why not see for yourself.

WHAT HAPPENS TO ME
IN CHURCH

By now we agree that Jesus Christ is the central Hero of the people of the church, the teachings of the church, and the Scripture of the church. But with all of this, why is it that we can go to church and not get a single spark of joy in an entire service? What if nothing happens?

Do we *expect* anything to happen?

Funny how many of us don't any more. Maybe we once did. But singing that same liturgy over and over again, hearing the same preacher in the same pulpit say so many of the same words, wading through the same hymns Sunday after Sunday — all this kind of adds up to a downtwist in our churchgoing.

It downtwists our mouth, so we walk into church like corpses going to a midnight meeting. It downtwists our hopes, so we go into church without expecting the Lord to brighten our tomorrow. It downtwists our bodies, so we loaf into our pews and sit in a stupor until the Benediction wakes us like an alarm clock going off in our minds. It downtwists our hearts, so we don't have the courage to take part in the worship of the congregation — "too much work!"

That's the price we pay for getting into a rut, isn't it?

Well, what else can it be but a rut, this regular, dull Sunday morning routine that half puts you to sleep before you get out of bed? After all, we're just human, aren't we? And humans are like that. They get tangled up in their habits.

Right. But do they have to *stay* tangled up?

We certainly would agree that going to church with the idea of just getting through it is about as exciting as playing dominoes in the school library. That kind of church has none of the excitement that we want out of a Sunday morning.

It's not the kind of churchgoing Jesus had in

mind for us, either. Once He grew really angry about some people who were selling souvenirs in the temple. "Is it not written," He cried, "My house shall be called a house of prayer for all nations? You have made it a den of robbers." (Moffatt)

Those words, "house of prayer," hold a load of meaning.

Prayer means talking with God, coming into contact with Him, pouring out ourselves to Him, opening ourselves to Him. "Where two or three are gathered together in My name, there am *I* in the midst of them."

You call *that* dull?

Yet that's just what we're doing when we doze through one service after the other. We're saying that the "house of prayer" is really a house of Tired Nodding Teen-Agers. And that kind of "TNT" will never explode anywhere.

What you want — what all young teen-agers want — when you go to church, is a solid touch of our Lord Jesus Christ. You want to reach out to Him with both hands and with your voice and your eyes and your ears, and you want to know He is doing things for you.

You want to know He has you in His mind too.

And you can be sure of it.

Worship is a two-way street. You never travel

it without meeting Someone coming the other way. Someone very much in love with you! — More than any human can love you, so He does *already* love you. And He can lift you each Sunday by the sure sense of His touch.

To worship is like taking a cold drink of spring water on a long, hot summer day. Or like looking out from a factory window to the night stars in the heavens. Or like seeing the smile of your best friend in the morning. Worship is all this, and a lot more.

Worship is refreshing yourself — with God.

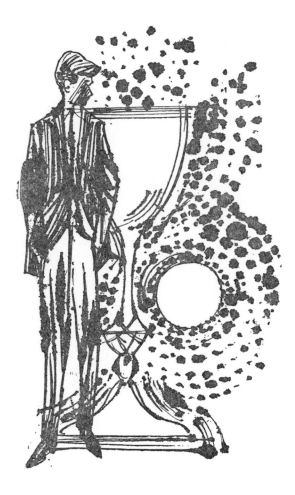

"I DON'T FEEL ANY DIFFERENT AFTER COMMUNION"

Jesus Christ is the Center of the Sacrament of the Altar.

You stand at the altar, drinking wine and eating a small round piece of white bread which has hardly any taste. You can't think of anything but the danger that you might drop the bread or spill some of the wine. And by the time you quit thinking of that you're walking back to the pew.

Maybe you say it after service, maybe you don't. But you — and all your buddies — are doing your share of wondering about it.

43

For the truth is, you didn't feel any different after Communion than before.

What's the matter with me? you say. Am I that bad?

Strange how easily we start accusing ourselves when something sacred doesn't live up to *our* ideas!

Believe it or not, there are a lot of people who feel "just terrible" when going to the Sacrament fails to touch their emotions. (And there are a lot of other people who make up for it by moving *themselves* into a first-class emotional state every time they step into a church.)

Without that thrill, they think, religion doesn't amount to much.

That kind of thrill-seeking hurts our going to the Sacrament. For we just may — maybe — keep on thinking that God is some sort of Supermagician who slips a mood over us just when we want Him to move us. And if He doesn't — nothing is happening.

Well, *is* something happening when you go to Holy Communion and don't feel a bit different after it's over?

Do you see the faulty connection we make when we ask that question? We pin God's acts onto our own emotional lapel. We say that *nothing happens unless we feel it happen.*

Imagine if we were to think the same way about an operation!

You are under ether while a surgeon takes out your appendix. You come to, see the cut, but deny that your appendix is gone. You didn't "feel" anything!

You might go through the rest of your days fearing you were still trotting around with a queasy appendix. But would your fear change the *fact* that it had been taken out once and for all?

Now try putting this idea to work on the certainty of forgiveness and of our Lord's presence, which the Sacrament brings to us. Something like an operation is happening here, isn't it? Our Lord is at work on us. His love for us, His death for us, His forgiveness — all these are *facts*. And He is using these as a scalpel to slice out the accumulated soreness of our sin, our pride, our selfishness. And deep inside He is rebuilding our faith.

Now, if all that depended on your *feeling* it, you'd be pretty badly off, wouldn't you? God would be just about your size, then — which wouldn't be too good for you or God or anybody going to the Sacrament. You really don't want a Lord that small, who runs sweet or sour according to the state of your digestion on any given Sunday morning.

You want a Lord beyond yourself.

You want Someone beyond your emotions.

And you have Him.

You can be glad that, even when you *don't feel* forgiven, you can KNOW YOU ARE FORGIVEN. Even when you don't *feel* His presence, you can KNOW HE IS PRESENT.

That is faith. And that is exactly what you want when you go to the altar. Not a happiness pill, not an emotional tug, but this: "I BELIEVE — EVEN WHEN I CANNOT SEE OR FEEL. YET I BELIEVE."

BAPTISM —
YOUR WAY TO BE SURE

Jesus Christ is the Center of Baptism.

Christians do not stop being sinners. They stay sinncrs. But they are at the same time just, righteous, holy, by the work of Jesus Christ.

We know that from our Catechism. But what does it mean?

Well, for one thing it means quite a lot of heart-searching.

You can't be sinning all the time without asking yourself some horribly painful questions. One is: "How can I be *sure* I'm saved?"

Because even a Christian's a sinner, he's going to doubt his own salvation once in a while. You find yourself doing it too, don't you?

That's natural. But it isn't God at work.

Because before you could even think, or remember anything, or feed yourself — before all this, God was giving you complete assurance that *you are His.*

It happened a long time ago. You were baptized.

What does it mean now? A certificate in a scrapbook. Something we talk about. But what does it add up to?

To Martin Luther, a great church leader (but one who at times still had his doubts about his own salvation), Baptism added up to PROOF.

It was proof of the power of God's Word, which acted through the water. It was proof to him of the love of Jesus, in whose name Martin was baptized. It was proof that Martin was God's child because in Baptism all — get that "all" — his sins were forgiven.

Sense? Or nonsense?

You get into trouble with your parents or your teacher. You feel down and out. All of a sudden you feel there's nothing you can be sure of any more. You think you're just a barnacle on the hull of society and the church and your family. You don't think of your Baptism — it seems a hundred miles to the rear, and you don't have time.

So many of us don't have time for the biggest things in life, because we're all wrapped up in the smallest. We tinker with alarm clocks and ignore the booming of Big Ben. We remind ourselves of our puny size and don't even glance at the looming shadow of our Lord hovering around us. Baptism seems just a drop of water in the ocean that threatens to flood over and drown us.

Really, we're talented at twisting things.

Baptism was no "drop of water" to Jesus Christ.

It was His way of reaching out to you before you could think for yourself. It was His first way.

And it was His permanent way. For the forgiveness of sins held out to you in Baptism is marked plainly: "Good Any Time!" In fact you actually draw on this covenant of forgiveness every breath you take.

Baptism shows us the real Jesus.

He can't wait to get to you, to help you, to stand with you. So He comes to you even before you're old enough to say His name.

Of course, circumstances make some of us wait until we're older. But even then Christ comes to us in Baptism in a way that remains mysterious and *wonderful beyond words*.

And even then it's good just to sit back once in a while, breathe deep, and say to yourself: "Remember, you're baptized. You're His!"

Because that's the way Jesus Christ works for you.

That's the way Jesus smoothes out your doubts and your fears.

He says: "I am *your* Way, *your* Truth, and *your* Life too. I am yours. Only believe."

And then He adds: "Be not afraid."

Remember? You're baptized! And that — just that alone — "works forgiveness of sins, delivers from death and the devil, and gives eternal salvation to all who believe this. . . ."

Do you *believe* it? Really?

I hope so. For right here your life starts!

IS IT TRUE — ARE THERE SNOBS IN THE CHURCH?

Strange that Jesus Christ seems to be missing in the lives of so many church people. Is it true, *are* there snobs in the church?

Yes, it's true.

"After all, just *look* at the nail polish she wears! I wouldn't be caught dead in the same pew with her!"

And she won't.

We all know people who move from church to church, something like shuttlecocks in a badminton court of crazy mirrors. "Social mobility," it's called. Which is why some Baptists join Episcopal churches. Usually they weren't good Baptists, and usually they make worse Episcopalians. But Episcopalians — "Well, they're just a little higher socially, don't you know?"

Then there's the inside-snobbery. This is the type that can make any Christian's skin crawl (if he isn't a snob). Rapid Rob Businessfellow joins First Christian Church because First Christian will soon build a spanking new church kitty corner to Rapid Rob's Rugs. Or there's the bank's vice-president, Mr. Smooth Soothemall, who knows that any good bank executive simply has to have a position in a respectable church.

What in the world could be more respectable than First Christian Church? Even Rapid Rob Businessfellow goes there — and you ought to get a sniff of his account at the bank!

Mr. Soothemall may have more than a sniff of Rapid Rob's bank balance, but he doesn't have much more than a sniff of what the church is all about.

Imagine Jesus patting Rapid Rob and Soothemall on the back and saying, "That's faith, brethren!" What's the matter? Doesn't the photo look real? Doesn't it match up with the picture the Bible paints for us — the one of Jesus congratulating the downhearted publican while He wondered whether the bragging Pharisee would ever accept grace? You don't need God much when you think you've done it all yourself, do you?

How much do you need God if you think you're cut at least a few notches higher than the rest of the people in your school or on your block or in your church? Are we being publicans or playing the role of Pharisees?

All of a sudden we're talking about "you" (and me, too) instead of the "snobs." We have to talk that way now — ever since we came to realize (last paragraph) that being a snob means simply thinking we're better than someone or anyone else. And that, we all have to admit, is about as common as horseflies on a horse.

In other words, we're all — in a little way, at least — snobs.

Look at a child, for instance. The baby in her crib cries when she's hungry or when she's wet or when she wants somebody to quick come play with her. She is all selfishness — even though she is all *cute* selfishness. Another child in the next crib could be choking on his Pablum, and our baby wouldn't care in the least. Just so there's a little Pablum left over for her.

There's a name for this selfishness, this concern only for "me." It's a most unpopular name. I'm almost afraid you'll leave if I mention it — its so old-fashioned.

It's called *original sin.*

That's the "I-me complex."

Or the "no one else-nothing else disease."

This complex, this disease, is under our skin the minute we're born. And it sticks with us until we die. And it shows itself in a blizzard of ways all the while we live with other human beings.

One of the ways we prove we still have original sin with us is by acting like snobs.

Snobbishness is selfishness going out and hurting people. It's Mr. Original Sin dressed up in evening clothes.

And there's only one way to deal with Mr. Original Sin.

We all need some outside help to keep him at our heels.

We need to know Someone else was *not* selfish but gave Himself up for us all, even going to the death of the cross.

When you know you're loved and forgiven like that, maybe you can forgive all the snobs in the church — and yourself as well.

And maybe you can keep Mr. Original Sin from having too many dates with you.

One thing is sure: our church can always do with a few more publicans and a few less Pharisees. You'll always have trouble liking a habitual snob — especially when it's you.

YOUR SALVATION —
PERFECT

Talk about both sides of the
church. The side where you can
see Jesus Christ and the side where
you can't — the good and the bad
of it. Yet in the end you have to
admit that Jesus Christ has made
our worst experience in the church
worthwhile.

He has done it all. He offers
us Himself freely, lovingly, and
eternally. Only a fool would turn
down such a gift or try to attach
strings to it.

But what fools even the best
among Christian teen-agers can be!

"It's amazing," said my camp director friend, "it's simply amazing, how many teen-agers think they've got to *do* something to be forgiven!"

"What do you mean, 'teen-agers'?" piped another voice. "Almost everybody I know feels that way."

This do-it-yourself animal can take on a dozen different colors, like a chameleon. There's the Christian who thinks you have to pray for forgiveness every day, or you're not forgiven. He's forgotten that you pray to get reassured of the forgiveness that always is yours.

Or there's the candlelighter or the bead counter or the bell ringer (up and down at 3:00 A. M. for a certain prayer for this or that). Or the driven churchgoer, who goes to services "because my conscience would kill me if I wouldn't, and besides, I've got to, or I feel like a heel all week."

Now hold on a minute. Is it wrong to go to church — or even to light candles or get up at 3:00 A. M. to say a prayer? Doesn't the Catechism say we should go to church and pray regularly?

It sure does.

But when you think that you "have" to go to church if you're going to "get" forgiveness, you're just about canceling out anything good that can happen to you *in* church.

Of course, you might feel better doing it that

way. You can go to work at this job, don't miss a service, pay 10%, keep the hours, run through the beads a couple times a day, and experience that zippy, tangy religious glow that keeps soothing: "You're all right, buddy. You've done it all."

There's only one thing wrong with that. It's self-centered, not God-centered. And your "self" makes a scrubby looking savior.

Our Lord never asked for us to be scrubby little saviors.

In fact, He went all the way the other direction when He said: "For by grace are ye saved through faith, and that *not of yourselves*. It is the gift of God, not of works, lest any man should boast."

That word "grace" is one worth underlining in red, white, and blue. It means free and undeserved love. It paints a picture of God handing His salvation to people without holding out the other hand to get a tip.

How would you like a God who had to have a person's money before He could give His grace to him? Wouldn't that be a puny God — just about the size of a midget compared with the real God and Lord of the New Testament?

All right, you admit, but there's a real problem here.

If we don't *have to* turn anything over to God to get His grace, what's to stop us from saying:

"I'll really go out and have a time — bum church, skip school, run a riot. God's grace is free, isn't it?"

Well, Paul beat you to that by about 2,000 years.

"Then what shall we conclude," Romans 6:1 echoes you. "Are we to continue to sin to increase the spread of mercy?" (Goodspeed)

Are we? "Certainly not! When we have died to sin, how can we live in it any longer?"

And there's the only real answer.

If a Christian still loves to sin, his love for Jesus Christ and His forgiveness is skidding downhill faster than a banana peel on a toboggan slide.

By taking Jesus into our lives we bet ourselves on Him. And in this game you can't play two sides at once.

It's hard enough to keep our one side straight and to keep reminding ourselves that our faith is based on GOD, IN CHRIST, IN HISTORY, OFFERING HIMSELF FOR OUR FORGIVENESS AND SALVATION.

But it's worth all the reminding we can do, this forgiveness. It's worth all the churchgoing, worshiping, singing, praying, and enjoying we can do.

Because there is no jewel more perfect, more beautiful in all the world than your salvation.

Wear it proudly. And don't be afraid to show it off.

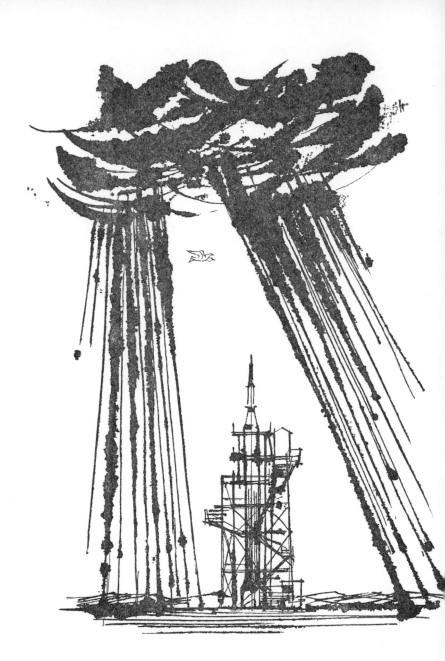

YOU WERE IN GOD'S MIND AT THE FIRST

Jesus Christ chose you to be a member of His church at the very beginning of the world, and His choosing you means that you should never be afraid of anyone or anything in the world.

"In the beginning, God . . ."

Out of the ooze, the slime, the dark — out of the empty eyesocket of earth — *God* . . .

"And the Spirit of the Lord hovered over the waters."

This was the creation of the world.

What we would give to see it

happen again! But there's no motion-picture reel on this, no news clipping, no photo. Not even a single witness to write about it or tell about it.

God, lonely and majestic, in the beginning started life moving and breathing in the new oxygen. Started the planets whirring in their orbits and the water rippling over a million falls all over the huge, round ball of world.

Yet, though we didn't see any of it, you and I were a part of it.

Adam was your father and mine, and Eve was our mother. And the earth we make our living from exploded into life during those fateful days of creating.

Six of them, six days, and the world was on its way. Toward what?

This is the question that disturbs Christian teen-agers when they think of the world.

"I feel," one of them wrote, *"as if there is a great deal of hatred in this world and that someday these bombs will be dropped and the earth will disappear."*

Or another teen-ager: *"It doesn't bother me in any way. Only when we have air raid drills, I get awfully disturbed and get a funny feeling inside of me."*

But *"it's silly to worry,"* another says. *"Every citizen should be prepared; everyone who can should take first aid. If God wills that we should be killed by a bomb, we will be."*

Bang or whimper — it's the end of the world when the bombs start falling, isn't it?

Most Christian teen-agers think it is.

It's perfectly natural to fear things like the H-bomb or a dictatorship across the sea or another world war. The very air we breathe is charged with the fears of all men. Scientists say that the air is charged with radiation too. Which leads any Christian to ask: *In all this, where is God?*

Could the Creator of the world actually let His work skid into this kind of mess? Can one or two dictators really destroy the world that the Lord Himself brought into being by His Word?

If this is so, aren't we saying that the lab has grown stronger than God?

Nikita Khrushchev said that Russians didn't need a god. They could create their own planets. And sure enough, Sputnik I seemed to be nodding his head as he twirled around the globe, hurling his teasing beep-beep-beep at ears which had never before heard anything from outer space.

There it was — a denial of God hooked up with a man who could wipe out life from the earth.

At least he thought he could.

What Nikita *couldn't* see — could never see — on the switchbox that sent Sputnik into the skies was a sign visible only to the eyes of faith: FIRE ONLY AT PERMISSION OF GOD.

Not even Nikita can do away with the Word of God, the opening blast of Genesis: IN THE BEGINNING, GOD! And it may be that in his deepest self even Nikita knows that the final epitaph of the world will have to be: IN THE END, GOD!

So let's get it straight. Christians are both right and wrong when they think that men can destroy God's creation.

Sure, it's possible — but only if the Lord lets it happen.

This means that the champion of all of us, our Savior, still holds the world at His fingertips. And He will always reign. He will always win. He will always win *for us*.

All that is written black on white in the story of the creation.

And all that is signed: *Yours, from your Maker.*

As for Nikita — next time you read one of his rantings, quote a little Genesis at him. See if it doesn't help you out.

THE COMMANDMENTS
CAN HELP YOU TOO

One part of the church that teenagers often don't like is the part that keeps telling them what to do and not to do. All this part is wrapped up in one section of Scripture, in Exodus 20. We call it "The Commandments."

Because we feel that the Commandments are there to stop us cold, we often find ourselves rebelling against them. We don't like to feel that we are so bad that we need rules to live by; or so uncontrollable that we need Commandments to control us.

What we forget is that the Commandments are there also to love us.

Take the Sixth Commandment — the one that teen-agers probably think the longest about — and look into its real meaning for you.

Teen-age crowds around the high schools whisper words about necking, petting, and "passion pit" practice at the drive-in. It's so often "the only thing to do."

If you're a girl, you do it to get dates. If you're a boy, you do it to have fun. And whoever you are, you go along to be popular — or (so they say) you sit at home and read novels.

On the other hand, there *are* quite a few Christian teen-agers who manage to hang on to, or recover, the Sixth Commandment long enough to make some kind of a Christian choice. *If I have to go along with the morals of the crowd to be popular, I'll be unpopular* until my kind of person comes along.

That kind of "un"-popularity brings together some of the cleanest, most upright fellows and girls you've ever seen.

"But," a voice protests, "but you should see how some of these *Christian* kids act on a date. They're just as bad as anyone — just going along with the crowd and sometimes leading the crowd into the worst of it!"

That is discouraging news, we'll have to admit. And no doubt it's true. Christian teen-agers long to be accepted by their group as much as anyone else. And often these Christian teens feel you have to let down almost all the bars to be accepted.

But what do these Christian teen-agers *really* want in a date? Don't they really want the security of being accepted? *Wouldn't it be something if all the teens who believe in Jesus Christ could feel accepted without doing things that hurt their conscience!*

Because — make no mistake about it — this "going along with the crowd" does leave scars, deep injuries. You simply cannot let your body be pawed over twice a week by two different boys and not ache in your heart the other five days. And if you're a fellow, you can't break through a girl's modesty and honor and hurt her conscience without calling yourself a heel when you get home from that date. Even if you don't call yourself one out loud, you'll know underneath that you *are* a heel. And that burns like fire.

In fact, there is probably no quicker way to tear down your self-respect and your joy in living than to play around with sex before marriage. That's why God said, "You shall not commit adultery." That's why Jesus said, "Whoever just looks at a girl with lust in his eyes has already committed adultery with her in his heart."

God was not giving commands just for the fun of it. He was protecting you and me and all of us. He was helping you to find something better in life than this heartache that always follows sex-out-of-bounds.

And there is something better. It goes by the old name of purity, which always sounds too much like "Puritan." But purity is not something vague and "goody-goody." It is something we need to live. Because there's nothing quite so good as feeling clean — either after a hot shower or after an evening out with your best friend or after the forgiveness offered and received in your church. It's even worth being "out of the crowd" for a while to have purity.

That Sixth Commandment wasn't written to hold you back but to show you a happier life. Take hold of it, pledge yourself to it, and say to yourself, "I *will* keep clean."

In the long run it's the clean teen-agers who find the dates and the friends who build, not destroy.

What other kind would *you* want — for yourself — for life?

"IT'S A DREAM
COME TRUE, BOB . . ."

God loves you with both Gospel
and Law. He can love you even
through the Sixth Commandment.
And in loving you the way He
does, through Jesus Christ, He can
make you able to love another person all of your life.

Loving is a word that says a
lot of different things to different
people. In a magazine ad I found
this romantic conversation:

SHE: **"Its a dream come true,
Bob. . . . I thought we'd NEVER
find it. Now we could almost
choose blindfolded — just by fol-
lowing our hearts."**

He: **"Looks as if BOTH our hearts are set on Lasting Spring — its a 'forever' thing, like our marriage!"**

No, this isn't spoken by two young things — one sweet and one heroic — at some glistening altar. And it isn't a conversation in springtime New Hampshire, with a dribbling waterfall and tender whispers puncturing the silence of two hearts vowing to love evermore.

Uh-uh.

This is talk at a silverware counter. This is talk about a teaspoon.

This is love shining in the gleam of knives and forks guaranteed to pave your road through marriage — and life — with love, joy, peace, an inner glow, and the bonus of eternal youth. If you're in the market for it, you might even get eternal life somehow through a coupon given with each set of marriage-making silver.

Do they *mean* it — these ad writers and dealers?

Sure they mean it, most of them. After all, they have to mean it. Or they will fail to sell the spoons — and then *they* won't have enough money to buy the silver that makes living today so jolly.

All of this believing in "the American way" can brew an awful acid stomach. And it does. Four ulcers is about par on Madison Avenue. It's rotten to have to put honey-sick words in the mouths of high school grads. But it's even worse to have to *believe* what you have to write.

And maybe it's still worse to *believe* what people write believing they have to believe what they're writing. Here lie the 99 per cent of us. At least sometimes.

Even in church we keep thinking of our pet interests — our car, our box ticket to the night game, our folding money. Our eyes wander blissfully to the dream boat up yonder. Someone is talking in the pulpit, but what does it matter? We're interested in living a *real* life, not a talking one.

Yet what the man in the pulpit is saying could change our life from the teaspoon-ad kind to the kind that we might only dream about now.

Would you trade? A life serving your car and house for a life serving people?

A forced smile at the teaspoon counter for a breathing warmth inside you at the certainty of your relationship to God?

A personality pulled in a dozen directions by this "Lasting Spring" and that — for a personality enflamed with a centered longing for one Lord, one Guide, one Friend, one Holy Spirit?

Do you buy the ad, or do you buy the life this man in the pulpit is trying to nudge into your fears and worries and wonders — the life of Christ?

"WHY AREN'T PEOPLE HEALED IN CHURCH?"

She had a point, the high school girl who brewed up a storm in our Sunday morning circle. "Look," she said, "at all the believers Peter healed, and John, and Paul. Why can't it happen today?"

Answer: It can.

In fact, it *does*.

You smile. Now you know I've gone too far. In all the years you've gone to church you haven't seen a single person healed of anything.

As for sick calls, not even your pastor claims that anyone's been healed by his prayers. You never even bother to ask him in confirmation class if this kind of thing ever happened. You wouldn't *expect* it to happen, would you?

But it does.

And here's the only nail we have to pound in. *It doesn't happen the way you think it should. But it happens!*

Did you ever, in the middle of one of those long, long sermons, turn your eyes to the congregation and scan the pews filled with your friends and your fellow members?

You're looking at a crowd of people whose faces look more peaceful and composed than they've looked in the last six days. These faces are relaxing in faith. The brains behind these faces are thinking of the anchor holds which their faith gives them. These are people setting themselves firmly in Christian doctrine, and living it already, and living it well.

These are people who are feeling the power of group therapy at its highest, group *healing*. For their faith is being fed by the worship and singing and confession of all the other Christians in that congregation. And over all of this interaction of faith looms the might of the Holy Spirit, sent to the church by Jesus Christ Himself.

There is enough healing here, enough of God's healing, to calm minds torn to shreds during the week by labor strikes, deserting children, job loss, sickness in the home, tiredness and boredom and depression. *And this healing is going on right now — even before the sickness has reached a crisis point!* This healing reaches through even to skin and bones — those bodies that need to feel rested before they can feel "rarin' to go."

God is reaching out to people through His Gospel, and God is insulating people against the onslaughts of life-in-the-rough. God is healing by keeping doubt and fear from destroying His followers. God is touching people — spiritually, mentally, physically. All this — and it is a week-after-week recurring miracle — is happening without noise, without a lot of attention. But it *is* happening.

Surprised? You shouldn't be.

How can nothing happen when Christ is around?

"Where two or three are gathered together in My name, there am I in the midst of them," He said.

That presence of His is just as powerful now as it was when He walked the earth visibly. He heals now just as He healed then. He comforts and strengthens now as He did then.

In your church groups this kind of blessing can take hold of you too. By keeping your membership with the church you open yourself to deep inner joy, a sense of belonging and peace that does wonders for your mind and your body. For your body and mind go together, not only to church but to the show or the gym or on that date where you just *have* to look alive!

But it's up to you to stay *open* to these miracles. Be with the people who accept Jesus as their Savior. Love them, sing with them, laugh with them.

Even if they can't talk about it, most of them know the miracle of healing together.

So can you.

BODY AND SOUL —
YOU ARE HIS

Your joy in belonging to the church of Jesus Christ changes everything in the world for you. For now that the full love of Christ pours into your soul regularly and with magnificent healing power, you are able to see happiness in the commonest moments of your everyday life.

Not so long ago I stood on a Colorado mountainside with more than thirty Christian teenagers. For weeks they had played together as energetically as only teen-agers can — diving into the camp swimming pool, whistling tennis balls and softballs and volley balls around, working riot in the mess hall, and building the healthiest tans this side of the Rockies.

But all this didn't stop them from coming together here on the slopes near Pike's Peak and singing just as energetically:

> Thee will I love, my Strength, my Tower;
> Thee will I love, my Hope, my Joy;
> Thee will I love with all my power,
> With ardor time shall ne'er destroy.
> Thee will I love, O Light Divine,
> So long as life is mine.

All this play not only didn't stop them, it led them to this real joy in their Lord. Suddenly they found themselves thanking their Lord for the happy health that only He can give — the warm understanding that only He is the Center not only of the Bible but of everything in life!

That "everything" includes sports, social fun hours, the big game nights at high school, and even the drudge days at summer jobs. It includes breakfast, lunch, dinner, dates, and sleeping.

Some folks seem to think that if you go to a movie, you're in danger of losing your Savior. If you dress too loud or laugh too long or sing your lungs out in the shower, you aren't "pious" enough or "serious" enough — for some people, that is.

To these people, life with Christ means walking around with a load in your heart and a Bible passage stuck on your mind and a look a mile long dragging down the corners of your mouth. They live in fear of going against God's grain. They think Christ hates smiles.

Then what did He mean when He said, "Be joyful"? What was He trying to tell us when He repeated constantly, "Peace be with you"? Is this peace or joy — to shuffle about looking for all the world like a corpse on leave?

No, those Colorado campers had the right idea when they combined their singing with their ball games. They were on top of a secret that many people never discover: the soul is part and parcel with the body. Build your body with Christian living, and you build your soul along with it.

That's why Christian teen-agers — if they really follow through on their faith — can become the happiest teen-agers anywhere. They have everything through Jesus: security, love, courage, confidence, freedom, and real wealth.

This is your chance to center your body building *and* soul building right in Jesus Christ.

Say it now: "Lord Christ, give me YOURSELF!"

With Him the world is yours.

LIKE A WALK
IN THE MORNING SUN

Before I close these chapters I have
to say another word about what
the joy of the church has meant to
me in moments when I have seen
the church's meaning most clearly.

The 8:10 bus from Washing-
ton, Missouri, stops at a corner
two blocks away. But I almost
always find myself walking another
half mile to the stone towers on
Manchester Road. I do it, I guess,
just to get an extra dose of the
morning sun.

Even in the middle of summer
the air hits you cool at that hour.

The gravel under your feet hasn't yet grown parched and hard. Missouri morning then seems as if it will last forever, as if the grass will never dry out and the white pavement never shimmer from heat.

It's at that hour of the morning that I can think best about what it's like to walk in the Christian faith. *Like walking in the morning sun,* I repeat to myself: *Everything clear and cool and brilliantly right!*

That's exactly how it is when you live "in the light of eternity."

Your road is shining white, and the sun bright but not too hot, and the air crystal cool, when you know that you are forever a redeemed son or daughter of God.

That fact — the fact of God in Christ, in history — lights up your life as surely as if your Lord had made the sun just for you personally. And sharply you see it all now: *I am not afraid!*

Morning sun. Light. Warmth and a refreshing feeling of belonging. Christians have used all these pictures and thoughts to tell others what it is like to be a Christian.

And all these pictures may be pretty, but they don't say all that's to be said. You can't capture the whole of Christian life and pen it up with a word. No cage can contain *life.*

You, for instance, know that you have forgiveness, full and beautiful and perfect. You can say: "How terrible it must be not to have forgiveness!" But can you ever really know?

Can any Christian ever really tell what it's like to die and wonder and fear where you're going — to hope against hope that *nothing* happens after death? I once looked into the eyes of a dying woman who had denied the Lord all her life. I tried to see what was in those eyes. And the thing I remember most is that I couldn't see anything except nothingness.

I guess that's what strikes me most about my walk in the morning sun.

For a few minutes I know what it is to be almost completely unafraid. The green mounds of spreading trees in the distance, the sweet-acid smell of cut weeds just off the road, the water drops in the thick grass, and the feeling that I belong there at that moment — that my Lord has given me this moment under the sun — all of it adds up to two famous words that Jesus spoke whenever He found His people in terror.

"Be not afraid," He said.

"It is I; be not afraid."

It's when that sentence starts to ring home that we know what it is to be a Christian. Then we start to see the white road in the sun, and we begin to sense the fresh breeze on our cheeks, and we know we need never be afraid again.

For what can we lose? Our lives? Jesus waits for us. Our health? Jesus heals us. Our joy? Jesus is our final Joy.

"It is I; be not afraid." All that you're learning, all that you will learn about your Lord, says finally: "Be not afraid."

Walk without fear.

Walk in the Sun.

YOU HAVE WINGS
TO HAPPINESS

Values higher than mountains of money, promises more precious than the Declaration of Independence — that's your faith!

Look at this array of values which your Lord holds out to you *free of charge:*

REDEMPTION — It's all done for you at Calvary. Don't try to add or subtract — just *believe, accept.* This is the stone on which all history turns — this event, this historical truth, *all done for you.*

SCRIPTURE — The solid and unshakable black-on-white record of God's love for you, His all-out sacrifice for you, His care for you always.

BAPTISM — Assurance and reassurance of the forgiveness of sins in Jesus your Savior.

LORD'S SUPPER — Here Jesus becomes a part of you and goes all the way again to tell you that you're *His*.

CHURCH — Under the Holy Spirit, His people together rejoice in their salvation, buoy up your spirits, repeat to you the fact: *God loves you!*

CREATION — God made this world — don't forget it. And God will decide what's to happen with it. Rest your cares in Him.

These, and all doctrines, lead to:

THE CHRIST LIFE: The most real, exciting life there is — a partnership with God Himself. *You* share your whole self with Him in prayer. *You* face every moment, every problem, every fear with Him at your side. *You* share Christ's victory over the grave.

Then — let's pray together:

Lord Jesus Christ, give us Your kind of life. While we live that life of Yours, we want to experience all the values of our faith — joy, love, confidence, hope, security, peace. More than anything else, Lord Jesus, we thank You for You.

100